BEAST MORFS

texts and designs
by Leonard Trawick

Cleveland State University Poetry Center

Grateful acknowledgment to the following publications, in which some of these pieces first appeared:

Assembling: "Ants," "Hey," "Ma and Pa Tucker," "Psst," "Sunday Mornings"

Chicago Review: "Easter X" "Head of Coleridge," "Locked Up in Tech High," "Psolyp," "Seven Sigils" "Some Books Are to Be Tasted," "Starvish"

Everyman: "Adventures of God"

Generator: "Awracknee," "Flicker," "Now," "Willowasp"

Poetry Cleveland (CSU Poetry Center, 1971): "Lenten Wedges"

Fifteen of the emblems in "Mab's Forest" first appeared as a chapbook, *Beast Forms* (CSU Poetry Center, 1971).

I: MAB'S FOREST

PEOT

SOLITARY BEAST ~ SECRETES INTRICATE FORMS WHICH DISSIPATE IN THE AIR

Flicker

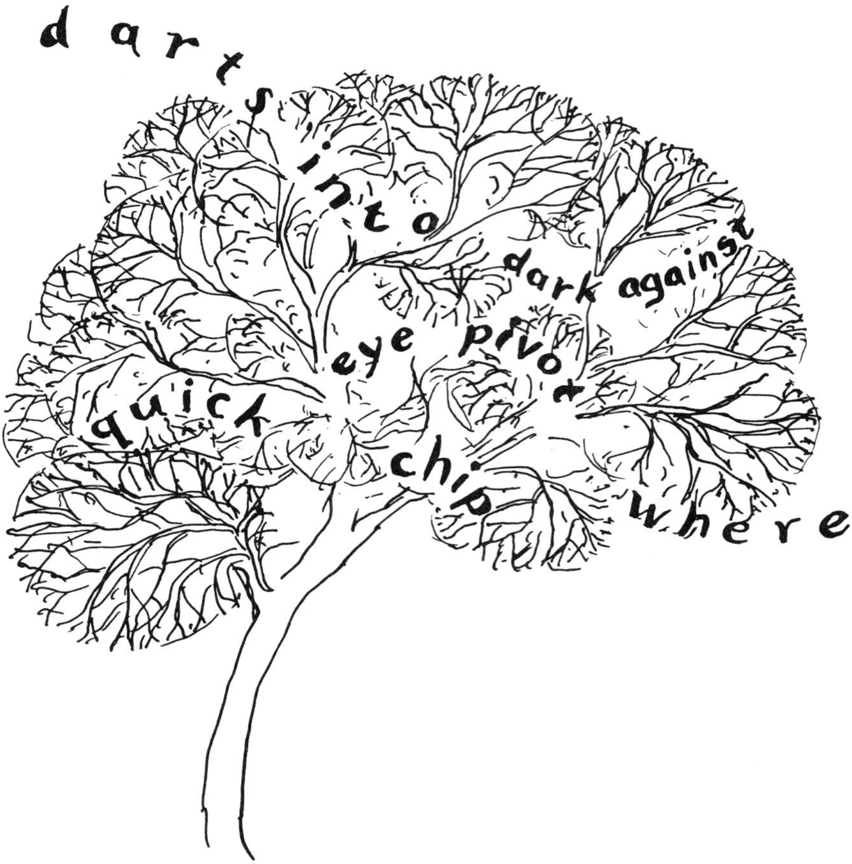

UNIPEG: a drill • a bore • an augury • transport of prophecy • μεταφορα • air truckin • soar feat •

psolyp

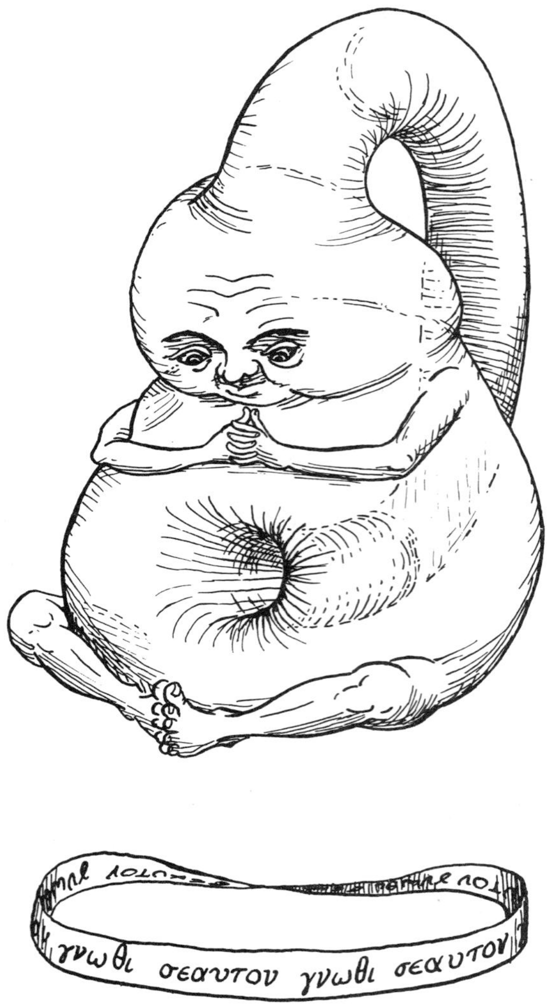

NIGHT BEES
come silent
to steal from our eyes
grains
of
the
day
for honey and dreams
SO BLACK SO SWEET

Butterfly Bat

Wings of neon nettle
Flitter against the retina

TOAD-MOTH
(4 a.m.)

CROAK
LURCH
STIFLE

Kudzoön

I bide.
Some day you,
so quick
and clever,
will doze.

cetus terrae

SPECTER

BLACK WINDOW

ROUND EYES

STALKER

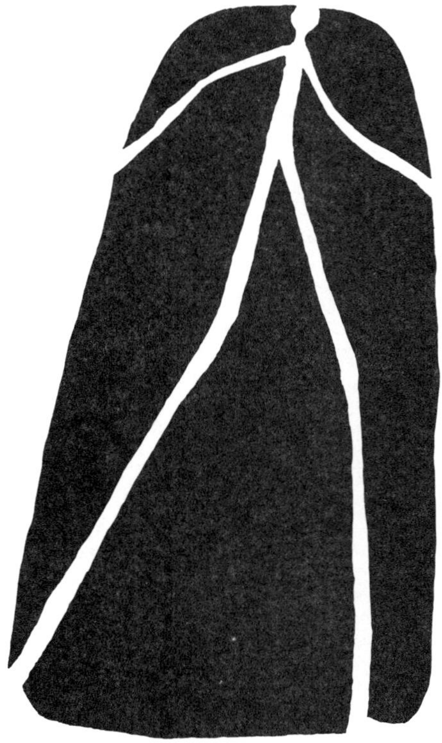

RISING FROM THE SLEEP OF REASON
DRAWN BY TIGHT SILENCES
AND ACRID SCENTS OF BOREDOM
FRETTING BORDERS OF DARKNESS
BATTENING ON DISSOLVING DREAMS

PROTEAZOON

SLIPPING BACK EVERY NIGHT

LIVID

WINK

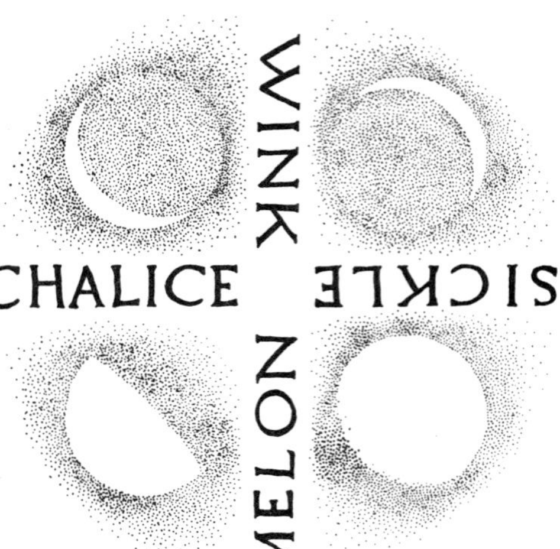

CHALICE SICKLE

MELON

Crystal Bird of Paradise

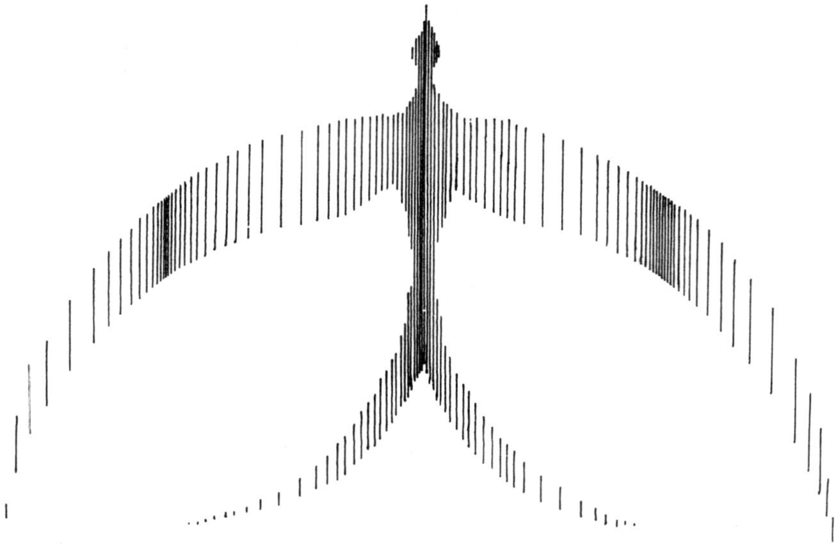

Flame quenched in sand ~ rainbow ~ too brittle to land

The World Toad
buffo mundi

all those unintelligible warts

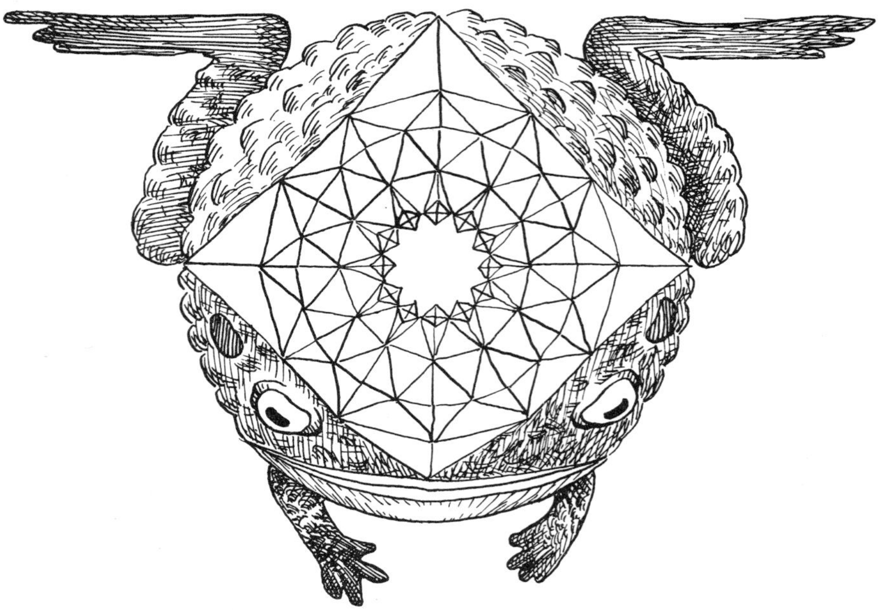

and that geode brain

☆

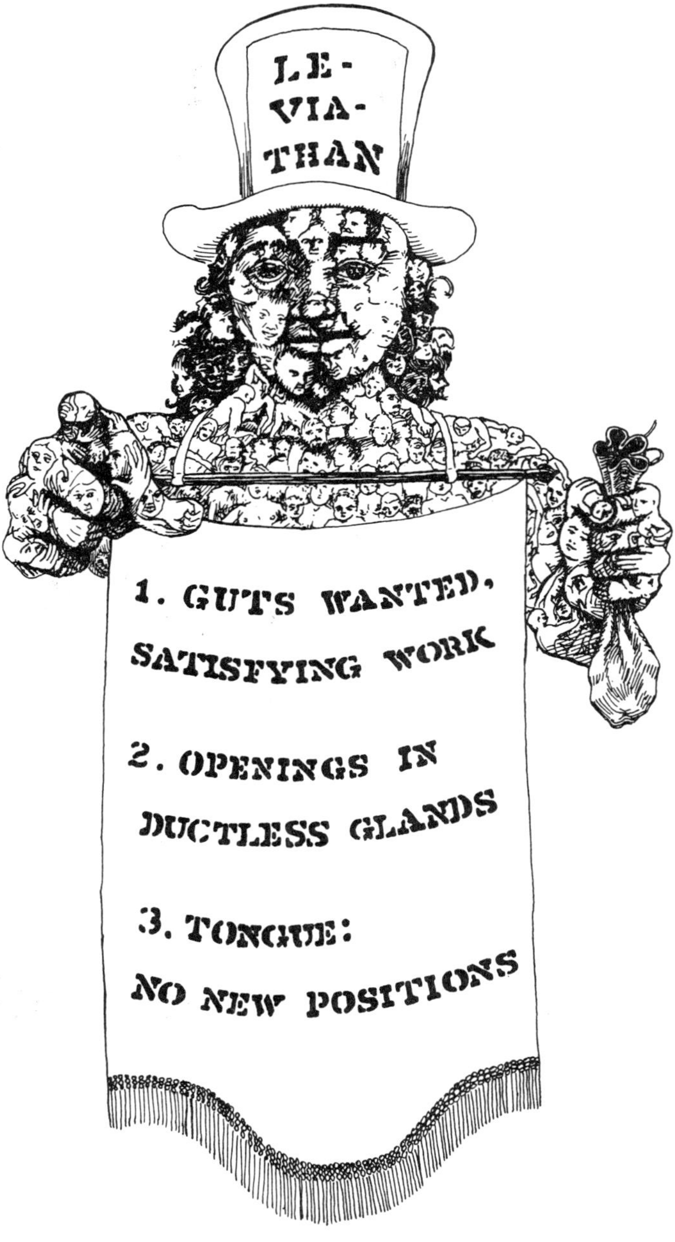
LE-
VIA-
THAN
1. GUTS WANTED,
SATISFYING WORK
2. OPENINGS IN
DUCTLESS GLANDS
3. TONGUE:
NO NEW POSITIONS

FYNGI

(little jokes of the night)

Willowasp

My garments
shed money,
ghostly fire.
Dead, I still sting.

AWRACKNEE

SIRENSPUNSONG

COMEDIE

STARVISH

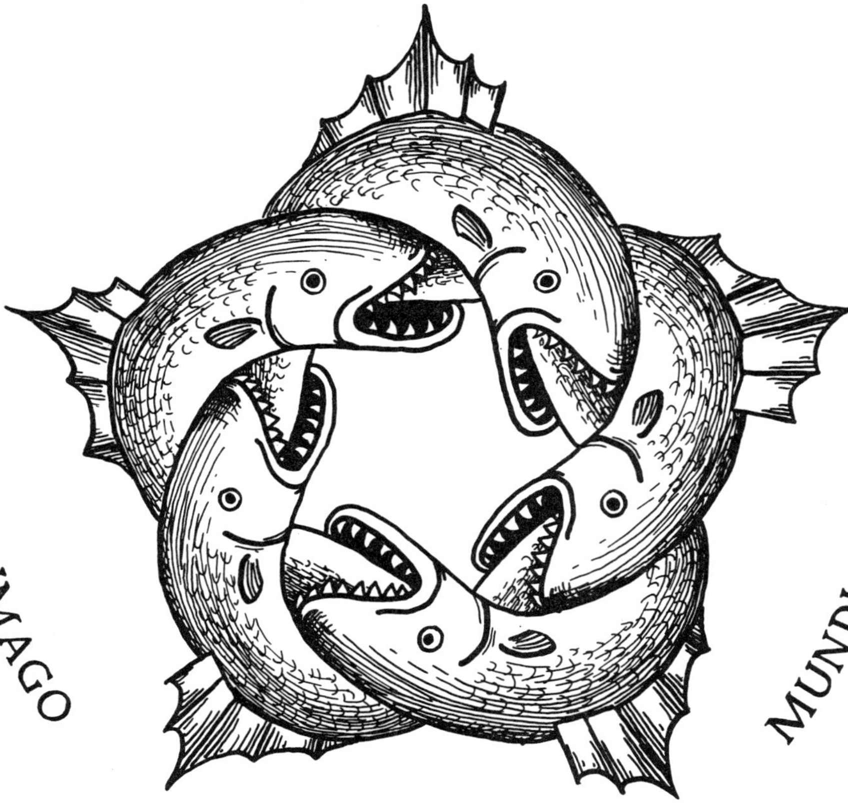

IMAGO MUNDI

INTEGRITATIS

Summer treeple: no misgivings

Winter treeple: no illusions

Urma

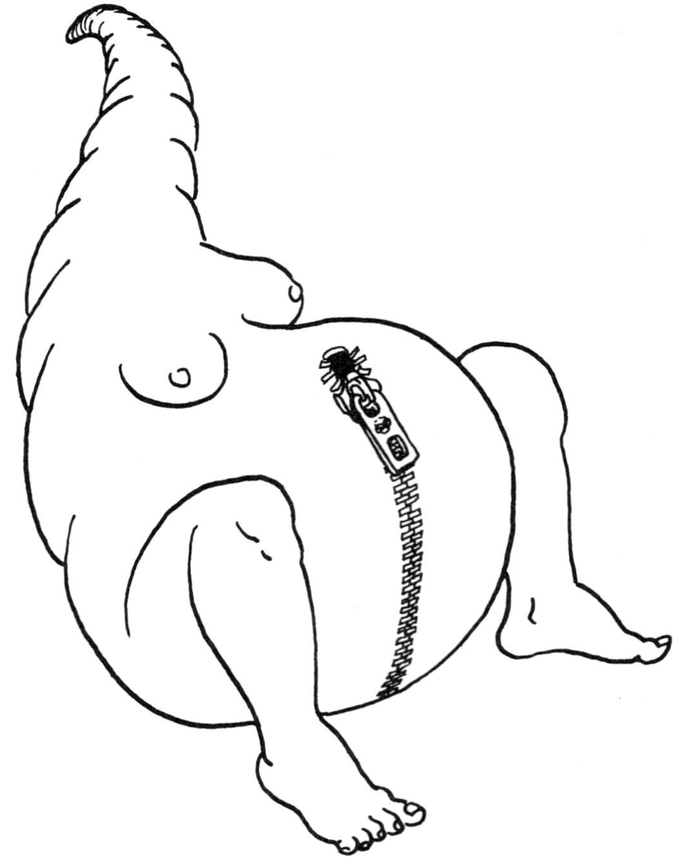

What face bears Fortunatus' coin?

Eurobore

mmoffs

wwaft mind mist

ssift shadow dust

pplush dream flesh

sshade-shift

sspin flaws into ghosts

BUMBERHEAD

"Like some fierce Mænad..."

SHELL I: PRUDENT NAUTILUS

BUILD THEE MORE SECURE MANSIONS, OH MY

Shell II: Butterfly

wave washed

stone wings

still flutter

wave washed

SHELL III: ORACLE

SEVEN SIGILS

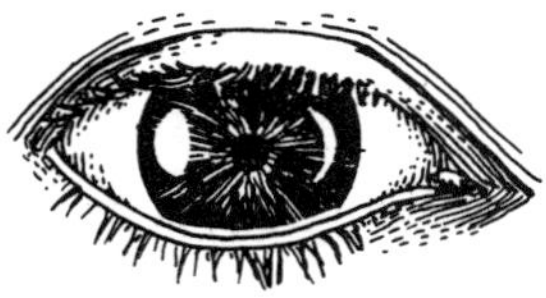

Mystic seals of the angels governing the days of the week (from Francis Barrett, *The Magus*, 1801).

Gabriel, barely waxed in luneship skewers

thorns, semaphores, daggers, flats, tides, clean to dele.

So soon, Camael,

fine points turn clubs.

It's a mill!
It's a grammophone!
It's the affable crank!

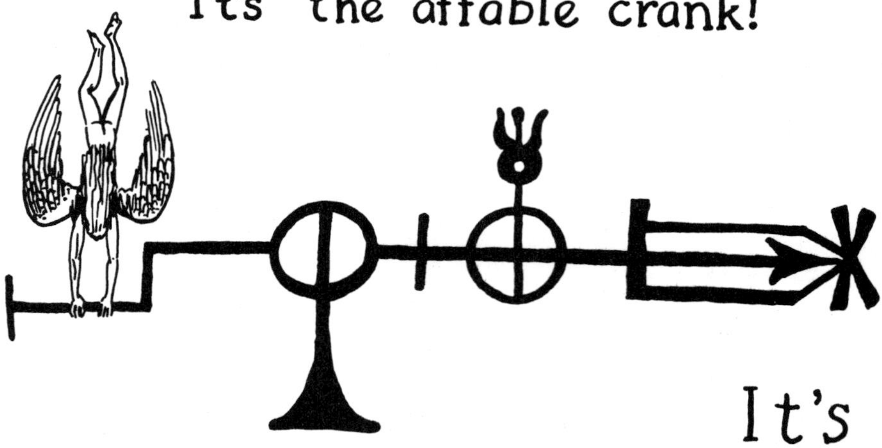

It's

over the hump
with Raphael's quick-
silver caduceus!

It should be thunderbolts, by Jove!

--but, oh, sad Sachiel,

Some Thursdays, no matter how you try, it just won't come out right!

A mouse
in a keyhole?

come
love day,

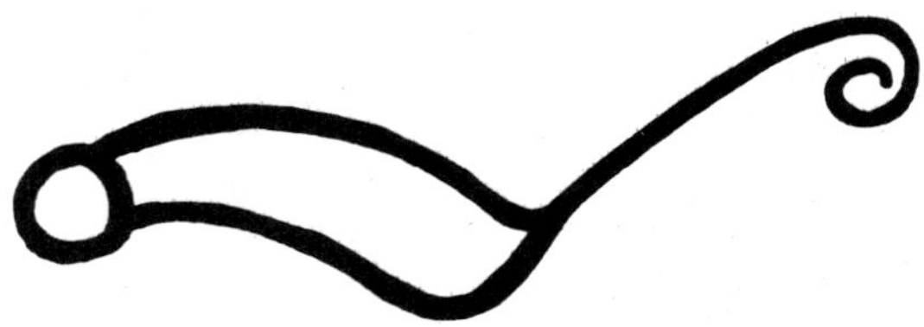

Anael's
martyrs doff such
kimonos.

Back with Cassiel

through solitudes and tears

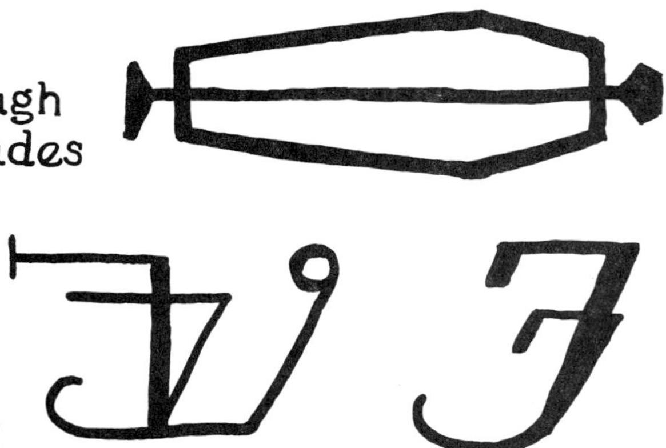

Again a salamander of the golden prime.

Michael sets eternally

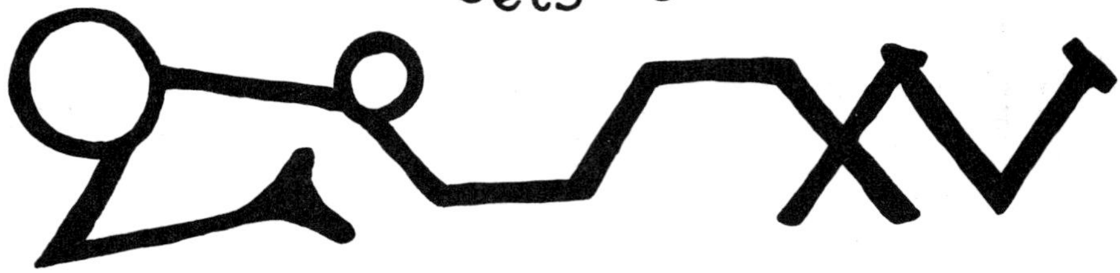

our chaise longue in the sun.

II: MOTES, BARFS, FROSTBEAMS

Some books are to be tasted . . .

LENTEN WEDGES

POOR SPIRIT BAFFLED BY GOD'S BOUNTY SULKS
IN CLOTH OF GOLD TILL STRIPPED BY GRACE
OF DEARTH THEN THRUST TO BLISS
RISES AND GROWS
MOST KEEN
WAX FAT
BURN OUT AND SOUL
SO MAY MY SMALL HOT SELF
SUBTLE AS VAPOR FAR AS LIGHT
SUBSTANTIAL TALLOW SNATCHED TO FLAME FLIES UP

OFF WITH GRANDFATHER'S GABARDINE PA'S SPATS
MY HARD EARNED BRAID NOW DANCE IN SELF
EXPANDING SEAMLESS RUN
FREE LEOTARD
OF SKIN
MY BONES
BEFORE GOD IN
I SHALL BE PROUD TO STAND
LAST ROCK HARD CLEAN TILL DOOMSDAY WHEN
THEY GROW KNIT SWIVEL MANUFACTURE BLOOD

Easter X

IN THE BEGINNING GOD VOIDED MAN
un us
Geist
O EVA A
O EVIL A
O VOID MAN · UOMO UOVO
WOMB TOMB
ROSEROSEROSEROSEROSEROS
Pêche
Pome
Poème de terreur
Odi Dio
LOГOS
EVO
VERBUM
NOAH
ARCUS LUNAE
YEAH
après vous, le déluge
je mords
je meurs
IONAH
Péché
Nato Natura
LOCO AMENS
I, Cain, am a maniac, I
So die, eidos!
Ai Θeos, I die!
Idea, adieu!
Able was I ere
I saw Erdu!
X
aos
PROPHETS OF LOSS
GNOSIS
TELLERS OF GUILT
ASSOIL US
RECOUNTERS OF FILTHY LUX
SI SONG
CON-
SOLUS
PETRUS
ERRANS
PÊCHEUR
ST. ONE
STEVEN
XRISTEROS
UNIVERSAL
PAN
CORP
He is risen
INDIVIDUAL
UVA
SANG
It is crushed
DIO
NISUS
A MORAMERDEGRACE
le mot juste
E LIVE
EVOE
O AVE
AVIS
ich
thus
HOLY
GHOTI
ROOD
Mary
Marry
Merry
Marthyr
MAN {WAS SAW} GOD IN THE END
AN INFINITE O IN SPACE

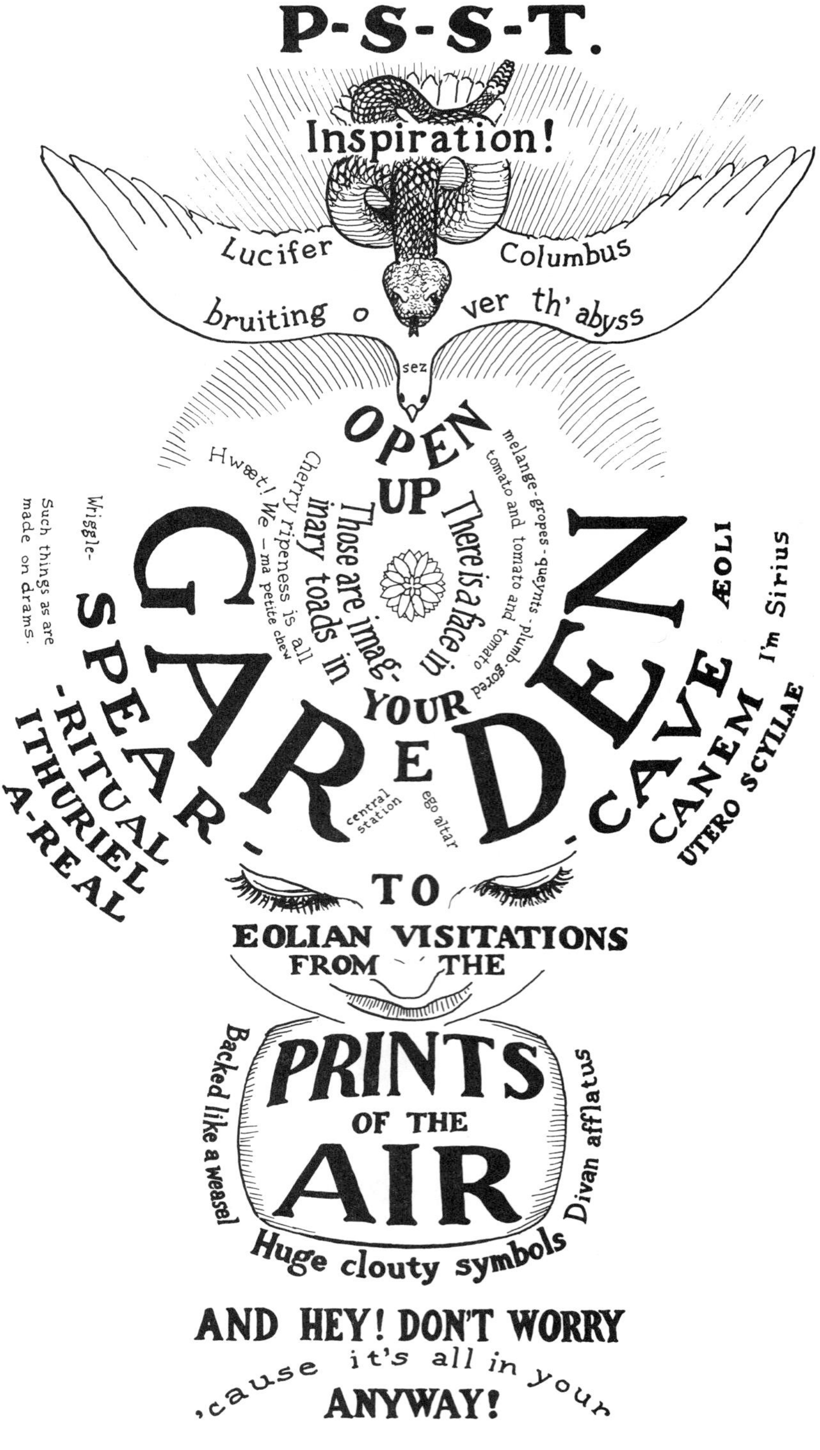
P-S-S-T.
Inspiration!
Lucifer
Columbus
bruiting o
ver th' abyss
sez
OPEN
UP
There is a face in
Those are imag-
inary toads in
YOUR
Hwæt! We — ma petite chew
Cherry ripeness is all
melange-gropes-queynts-plumb-gored
tomato and tomato and tomato
GAR
E
DEN
central station
ego altar
Wriggle-
Such things as are made on drams.
SPEAR-
-RITUAL
ITHURIEL
A-REAL
-CAVE
ÆOLI
CANEM
UTERO SCYLLAE
I'm Sirius
TO
EOLIAN VISITATIONS
FROM THE
PRINTS
OF THE
AIR
Backed like a weasel
Divan afflatus
Huge clouty symbols
AND HEY! DON'T WORRY
'cause it's all in your
ANYWAY!

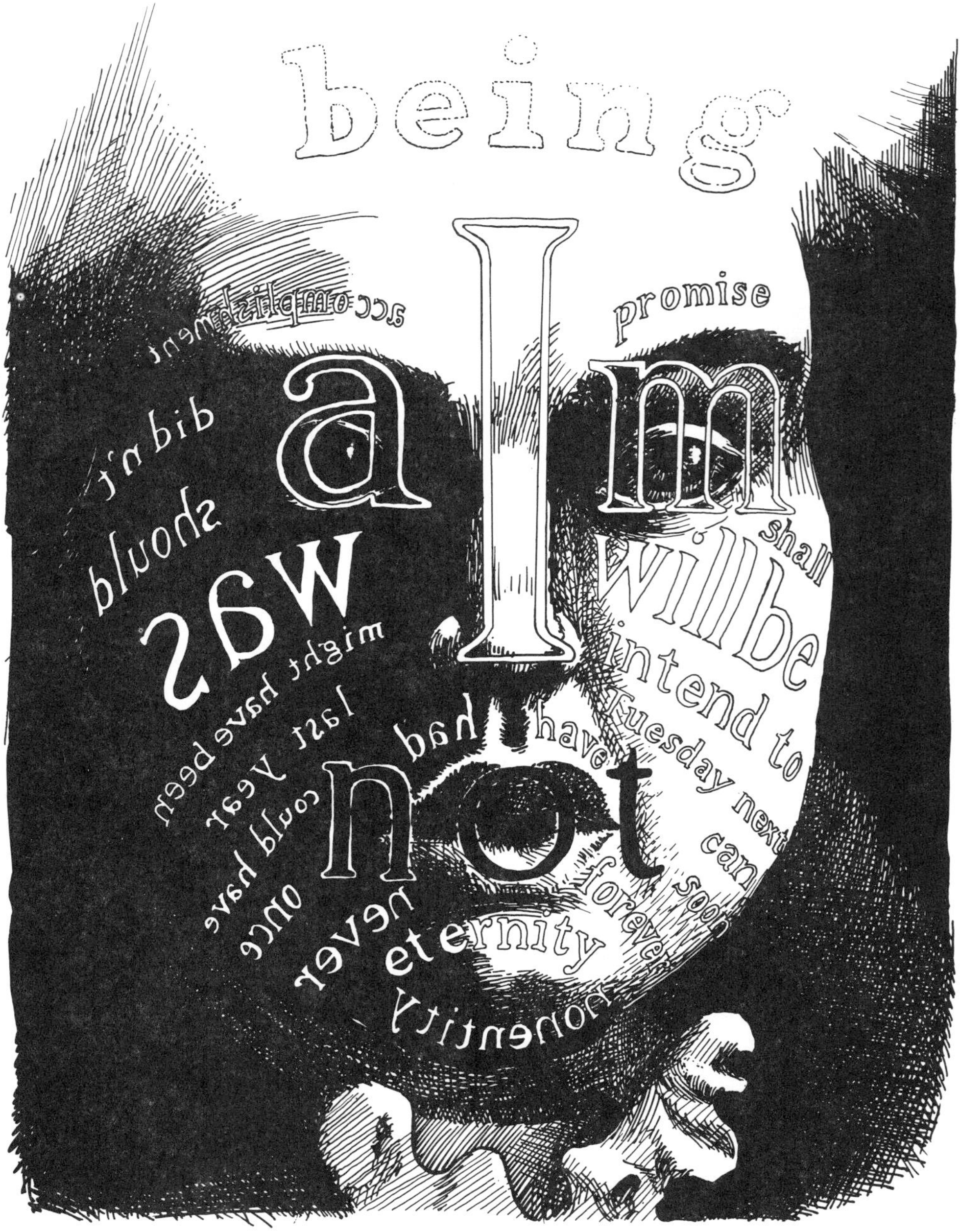

Head of Coleridge

HEY!
HEY BUCKA DOON I KNOW YOU OUT THERE YOU TROMPED DOWN MY FLOWERS
YOU STOLE THE MEAT OUT MY SANWICH YOU TOLD THE BOSS I WAS NOCOUNT
I KNOW ITS YOUR HAND ON THE DOORKNOB I'VE HAD ENOUGH BUCKA DOON
I'M CALLING THE POLICE I'M REACHING FOR THE PHONE RIGHT NOW
HEY BUCKA DOON SLOW DOWN A MINUTE
I AIN'T GOING TO KEEP ON DODGING YOU ALL OVER TOWN
WHAT YOU GOING TO DO IF YOU CATCH ME?
WE COULD WORK OUT A DEAL BUCKA DOON
YOU AND ME COULD BE OF MUTUAL BENEFIT TO EACH OTHER
YOU STOP CHASING ME
AND I'LL STOP RUNNING FROM YOU
HEY
PUT DOWN THAT HATCHET BUCKA DOON
DON'T CUT OFF MY ARMS, I CAN'T HOLD A JOB
DON'T CUT OFF MY LEGS, I CAN'T STAND UP TO NOBODY
DON'T CUT OFF MY BODY
I GOT TO HAVE SOMETHING TO KEEP MY MIND ON
HEY YOU KNOW WHAT BUCKA DOON YOU DONE OUTFOX YOURSELF AT LAST THERE AIN'T NOTHING YOU CAN DO TO ME ANY MORE

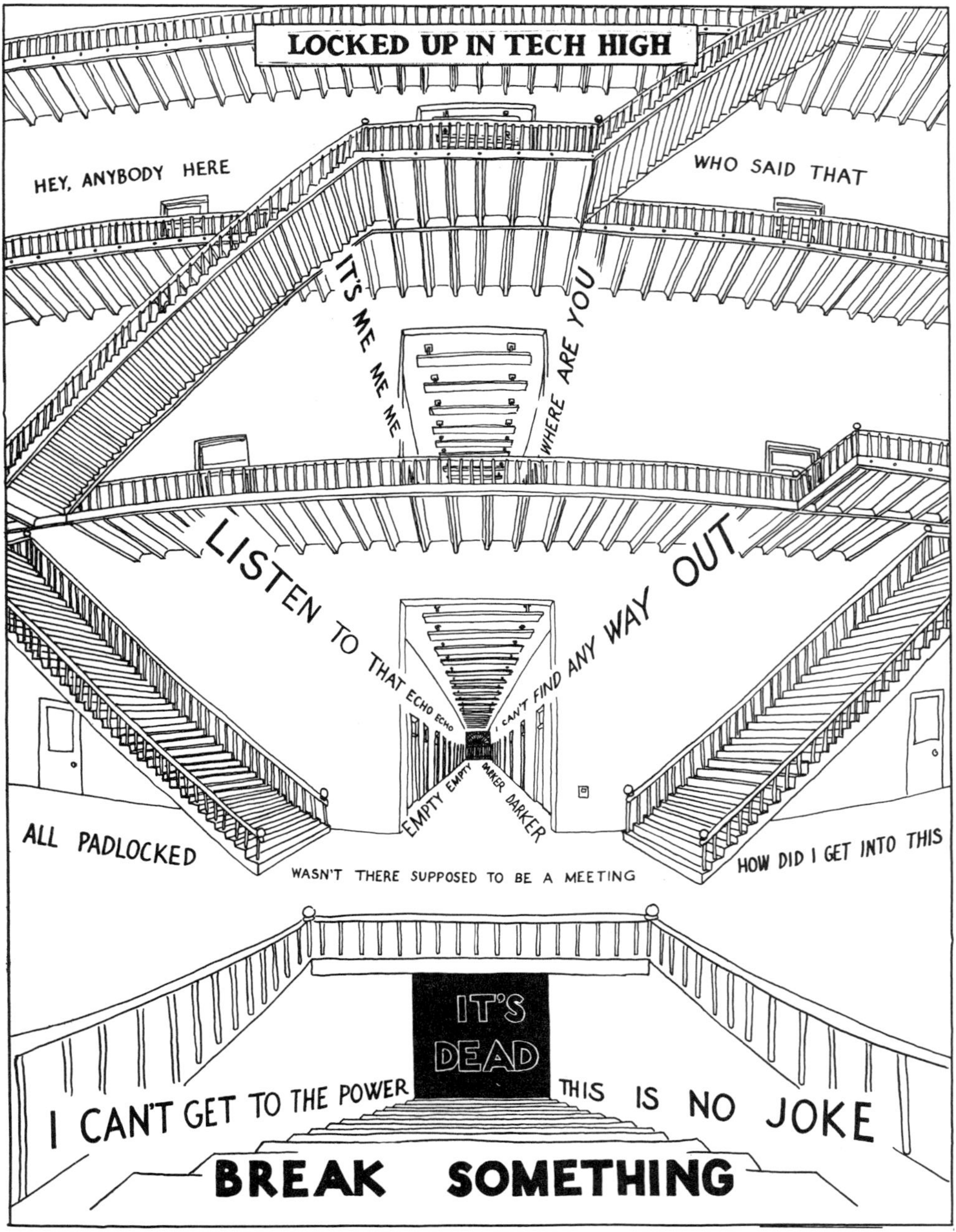

LOCKED UP IN TECH HIGH
HEY, ANYBODY HERE
WHO SAID THAT
IT'S ME ME ME
WHERE ARE YOU
LISTEN TO THAT ECHO ECHO
I CAN'T FIND ANY WAY OUT
EMPTY EMPTY
DARKER DARKER
ALL PADLOCKED
WASN'T THERE SUPPOSED TO BE A MEETING
HOW DID I GET INTO THIS
IT'S DEAD
I CAN'T GET TO THE POWER
THIS IS NO JOKE
BREAK SOMETHING

ANTS.

ANTS ARE BORN GROWN-UPS

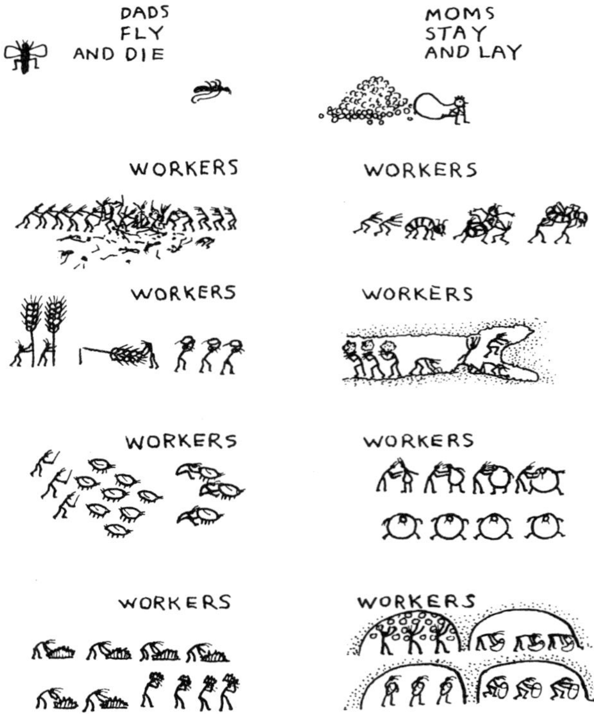

EVERY NOW AND THEN FOR NO APPARENT REASON AN ANT WILL WANDER AWAY FROM THE HILL AND

NEVER BE SEEN AGAIN

Nocturne

Largo

Now

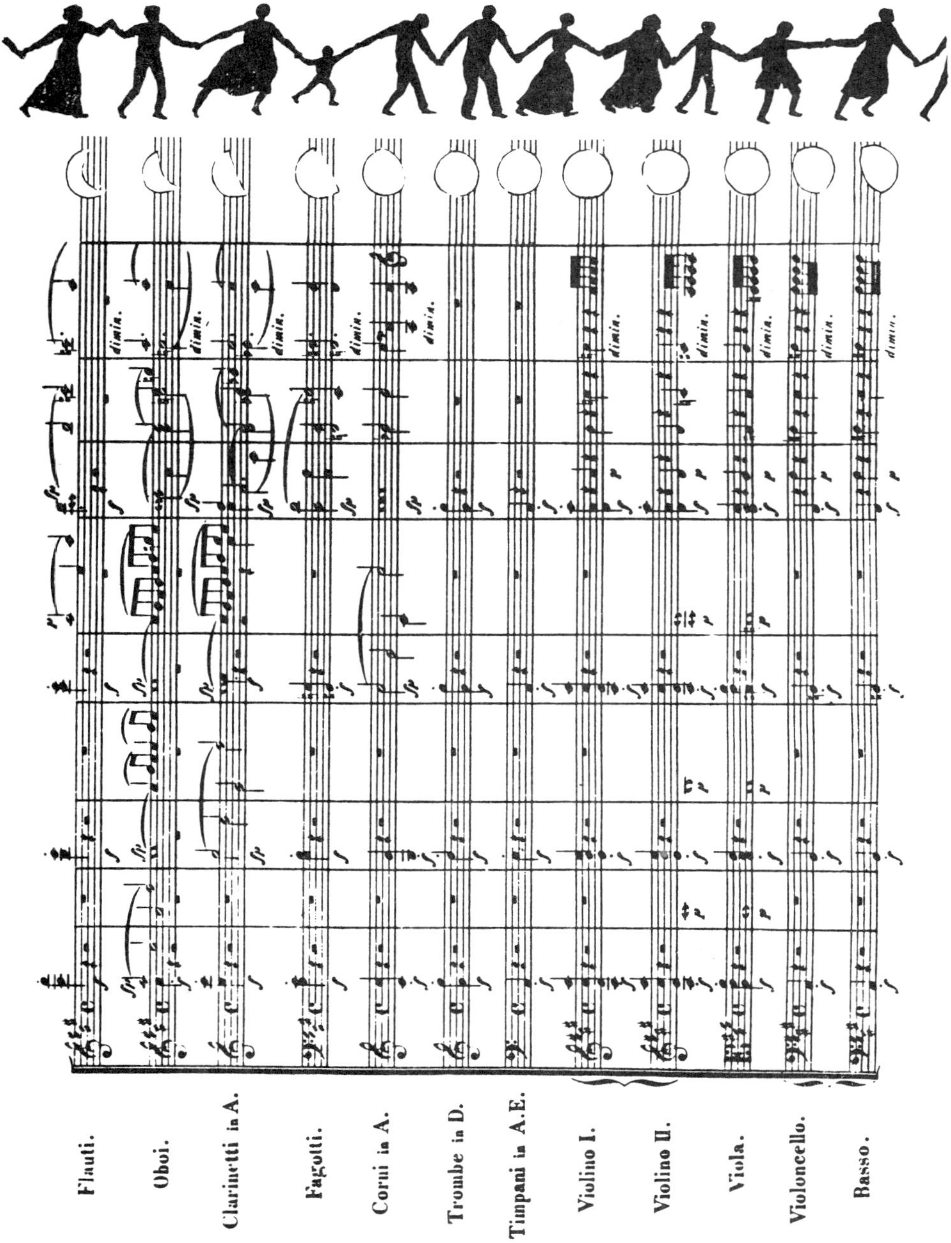
Flauti.
Oboi.
Clarinetti in A.
Fagotti.
Corni in A.
Trombe in D.
Timpani in A.E.
Violino I.
Violino II.
Viola.
Violoncello.
Basso.
dimin.

Now everybody join in the grand old song of

MA AND PA TUCKER

1.

Old Ma Tucker likes to rock you along,
She props you in the cradle and croons you a song;
When you're all tuckered out and ready for bed,
She tucks those covers right over your head.

Oh won't you tuck away, oh won't you tuck away,
Oh won't you tuck away these weary bones.

2.

I tuck my kit fiddle under my chin
And play pea-turkey till the cows come in,
And Old Ma Tucker just laughs like sin,
Cause she knows she's going to get to
tuck me in.

Oh won't you, etc.

3.

Old Pa Tucker he lives by the spade,
He deals out dirty till you're over your head;
He's all booked up till Judgment Day,
And he's waiting pretty baby just to
tuck you away.

Oh won't you, etc.

4.

Little Sis Tucker is a tuckin' fool,
She'll tuck in a truck or in a swiming pool,
But, brother, tuck your tail and leave that scene
When you hear Pa coming with his
tucking machine.

Oh won't you, etc.

5.

I went to the Ocean when the day was done,
The water was laughing, come and have some fun;
And I said, as a wave folded over me,
It's Mother Tucker tucking me into the sea!

Oh won't you, etc.

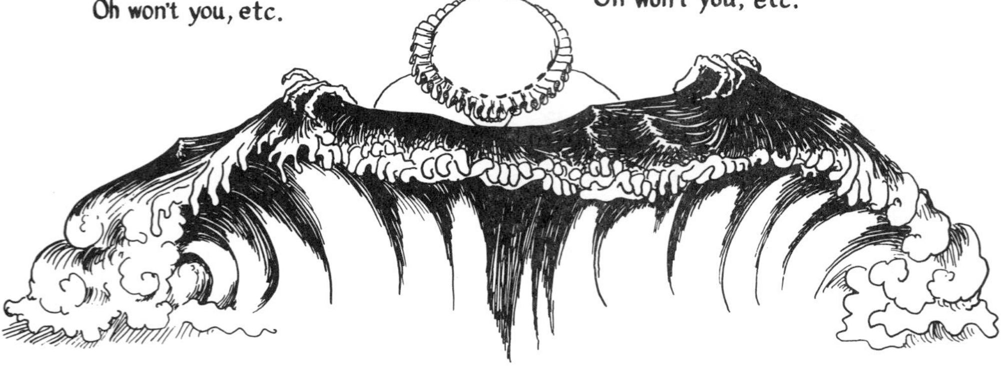

DIVINE COMIX

THE ADVENTURES OF GOD
EVERYONE IS SO NICE!
TRUST
HERE, KID, TAKE DIS!
GEE, THANKS!
EVIL
DIS-
TRUST
ALAS, NOW MY DAYS ARE POISONED!
DISTRUST
TRA-LA-LA! I AM A PART OF THE COSMOS!
THING
SAY BUDDY, THERE'S A LOT YOU NEED TO NO!
EH?
EVIL
NO-
THING
SNIFF I FEEL LIKE SUCH A NONENTITY!
nothing
HEY, YOU'RE TWISTING EVERYTHING AROUND TO MAKE IT LOOK BAD!
SO?
GOD EVIL
I'LL FIX YOU!
AWP!
GOD
WOW! WHAT IS THIS NEW VITALITY I FEEL? I'VE TURNED MY LIFE AROUND!
LIVE
ANOTHER CASE RESOLVED! ARF, ARF!
DOG

The Adventures of GOD
WHAT'S THE MATTER, CAN'T YOU FIND ANY WORK?
NO! OCCUPATIONAL OPPORTUNITIES ARE SCARCE --AND THESE BOILS SURE DON'T HELP!
GOD
JOB
JUST BE PATIENT-- A SUITABLE SLOT IS BOUND TO OPEN UP!
I AM CERTAINLY EAGER TO BE ENGAGED IN SOME REMUNERATIVE VOCATIONAL PURSUIT!
GOD
JOB
PERHAPS I COULD BE OF ASSISTANCE TO YOU IN LOCATING EMPLOYMENT!
I WOULD BE GRATEFUL FOR ANY AID YOU COULD RENDER ME IN LANDING A POSITION!
GOD
JOB
WHAT AREAS OF ENDEAVOR ARE YOU COMPETENT IN? CANST THOU BIND THE SWEET INFLUENCES OF THE PLEIADES, OR LOOSE THE BANDS OF ORION? CANST THOU DRAW OUT LEVIATHAN WITH AN HOOK?
NO-- I MAJORED IN BUSINESS ADMINISTRATION!
GOD
JOB
YOU SEEM TO HAVE A GENIUS FOR SUFFERING!
YES, BUT IT TAKES A LOT OF PRACTICE TOO!
GOD
JOB
SUFFERING'S A GROWING FIELD, WITH MANY DIVERSIFIED APPLICATIONS IN EVERY WALK OF LIFE! AMATEUR GROUPS ARE SPRINGING UP EVERYWHERE!
HOORAY! AT LAST I'VE FOUND MYSELF!
GOD
JOB

The Adventures of GOD
SAY GOD, IF YOU CREATED ME IN YOUR OWN IMAGE, ARE THE CHINESE AND AFRICANS CREATED IN THE SAME WAY?
YES, ADAM, I ACCOMMODATE MY IMAGE TO THE MANIFOLD LIMITATIONS OF HUMANITY.
TO THE GREEKS, I APPEAR AS A MAGNIFICENT GREEK...
...WHEREAS FOR AN ASIAN I REFLECT DIFFERENT SPIRITUAL IDEALS.
YOU MEAN IT'S ALL DONE WITH MIRRORS?
YOU MIGHT PUT IT THAT WAY.
YOU SEE, YOUR IMAGE OF ME IS A PROJECTION OF THE TRAN-SCENDENTAL SPIRIT IN YOU.
IN OTHER WORDS, I AM THE CREATION OF MY OWN SELF-PROJECTION!
IN A MANNER OF SPEAKING —YES.
HOORAY! GOD IS DEAD!
A-A-A-K
TSK, TSK! AMAZING HOW A LITTLE METAPHYSICS ALWAYS DOES THEM IN!

SUNDAY MORNINGS

LONG AGO, WHEN POPEYE FELT 

AND THE BLUE GOON SAID, 

AND INTO SWEE' PEA'S MIND FLASHED 

THEN !! 

AND GEEZIL SLUNK OFF MUTTERING  # @  !!

—MY DADDY READ THE FUNNIES SO .

(EVEN WHEN HIS BREATH 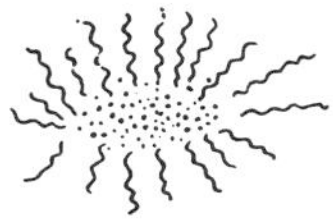)

—HE WAS , IT WAS REALLY 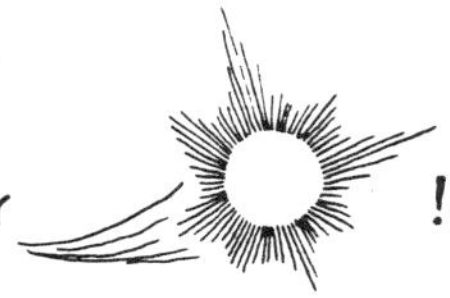 !

AND EVEN NOW, THOUGH MY DAYS ,

MY BREAD , AND MY BEER ,

IN SPITE OF , , AND ,

WHEN I OPEN THOSE SUNDAY FUNNIES, !

IT'S JUST